Act More like a Boss

Six main knowledge and skills for rising female CEOs

By

Katty k. Young

Copyright © by Katty k. Young 2022. All rights reserved.

Before this document is duplicated or reproduced in any manner, the publisher's consent must be gained. Therefore, the contents within can neither be stored electronically, transferred, nor kept in a database. Neither in Part nor full can the document be copied, scanned, faxed, or retained without approval from the publisher or creator.

Table of content

Introduction

Chapter 1
What factors contribute to a person's level of success?
Chapter 2
Common challenges for leaders to face
Chapter 3
Conquering your own self-doubt and the imposter syndrome
Chapter 4
Building self-confidence in yourself and your team
Chapter 5
Regain Control of Your Time and Energy
Chapter 6
The common strategies used by the most successful women in the world
Conclusion

Introduction

Do you label yourself a female entrepreneur? Do you have the tenacity to launch a company and become the dominant force in your industry?

For many young and brilliant individuals, the aspiration to be their

own boss and to turn their hobby or interest into a paying vocation is becoming an increasingly common goal. Emancipation has led to an increase in the number of people, particularly women, who are willing to start their own companies and demonstrate their worth in a commercial sector that is still dominated by males.

In point of fact, female entrepreneurs in the United States controlled more than 11 million businesses in 2017, which together accounted for 9 million jobs and 1.7 trillion dollars in sales. Not only is there a surge in the number of women starting their own businesses in the United States, but the number of successful female entrepreneurs is on the rise all over the world.

However, the reality is that a large number of women are interested in launching their own businesses but are unsure of

how and where to get started. Some people who had the courage to begin ultimately failed after just a relatively short period of time. Although becoming an entrepreneur is seldom a walk in the park, we want to inspire young women to believe in themselves and trust their decisions as they embark on this one-of-a-kind and fascinating adventure.

You will find that reading this book is of great assistance to you.

Chapter 1

What factors contribute to a person's level of success?

What is it that sets successful individuals apart from others? What are the characteristics that are shared?

It seems as if everyone wants a piece of the pie when it comes to leading a successful life. Everyone has the same goal in life, which is to achieve the highest level of success possible for themselves.

Regrettably, there are not many people in our world who can claim to have actually attained exceptional accomplishments in their lives. And because of this, attaining success is an accomplishment that is much more valuable.

It doesn't matter whether you want to be successful in your work, in your company, in your investments, monetarily, spiritually, or in your role as a family member; you must first decide that you desire success in order to achieve it in any of these areas.

The majority of individuals are not dedicated, and they lack the courage to make a choice to work hard to achieve what it is that they want out of life.

Learn how to take advantage of the principle of attraction.

Only when you are totally dedicated to achieving your goals and have made the decision that you will do so regardless of the circumstances will you see success.

So, what is it that sets successful individuals apart from others? What do they do that individuals who live normal lives don't do that allows them to enjoy such an extraordinary life?

There are 5 Common Characteristics that Set Apart the Exceptional from the Regular.

1. People Who Are Successful Have Ambitious Dreams

Yes, I am well aware that you have been exposed to this at least one million times. Nevertheless, I only like to stress to you one more time that individuals who are successful have ambitious goals.

The majority of individuals do not live the lives of their dreams because they do not have the courage to dream really large. In point of fact, most individuals do not dream very big. They just want to be happy; they just want to make ends meet; they just want to be able to pay the bills, etc., etc., etc.

If you shoot for the moon while aiming for the stars, you will at least make it there. It is unfortunate that the majority of individuals do not even shoot for the ceiling; thus, it is not surprising that they do not achieve outstanding success in life.

Get yourself out of the ordinary and into the exceptional as your first step toward having a great life. This is the first thing you need to do if you are serious about leading a successful life. And the only way to do this is to first think on a grand scale.

It is necessary, to begin with your own thinking. Your way of thinking will determine the course of your life. If you constantly focus on becoming successful, you will eventually get there. On the other hand, if you constantly dwell on the fact that you have failed and been defeated, you will never rise beyond mediocrity. Your ideas will become your reality.

2. Successful people are always going in new directions.
Do you know that in addition to having an expansive mindset, successful individuals are always on the move? They are the kind of individuals that don't sit around and wait for things to happen; rather, they go out and make things happen.
You are required to act in the same manner. Put your plans into action so that your goals may become a reality. There are a lot of individuals who have the desire to be successful, but they are unwilling to put in the effort necessary to make their goals a reality.
They will say that they want to be wealthy, that they want to develop a great company, that they want to own a large home, and that they want to drive a fancy automobile, but they are unwilling to put in the effort necessary to achieve their objectives.

Don't ever allow anything like that to happen to you. We are all aware that leading an amazing life is not a simple task, but the ability to do so is what differentiates successful people from others who lead conventional lives.
You should make it a daily commitment to carry out at least five easy steps that will get you closer to achieving your objectives. Even if you are only able to do five simple tasks

each day, you will have accrued 1,825 micro achievements at the end of the year.

And doing so will unquestionably produce the results you're looking for. Success takes consistency. Therefore, maintain consistency and act on a daily basis.

3. People that are successful will never give up on themselves.

When you look at the lives of great individuals who have generated fantastic results in life, people like Walt Disney, Colonel Sanders, Richard Branson, Michael Jordan, Jack Ma, and others, you will see that they just refuse to give up. This trait is what made them successful.

The road to success is arduous, and along the way, you will experience a significant number of defeats and obstacles. Nevertheless, you should never allow them to get you down.

You need to have the self-assurance to move on and transform your setbacks into opportunities for growth.

Great individuals never give up, and they never give up on the ambitions they've had for themselves. They will not give up and will keep working hard even when everyone else tells them that what they want to achieve is unachievable.

4. Successful people always have a positive outlook and expect good things to happen.

After reading success tales written by great individuals from all over the globe, I came to the conclusion that successful people have an optimistic attitude at all times and anticipate good things will occur in the future.

Consider the following: if Steve Jobs did not believe that his devices would be successful in the marketplace, do you think he would have gone ahead and introduced the iPhone or iPad? Do you believe that Richard Branson would launch a new airline despite the fact that he is always pessimistic and has a pessimistic outlook on the market and the economy?

They have a high level of confidence in what they do, and, as a result, they do not doubt the viability of their company or the products or services they provide. Because of this, they are able to keep going and put in an exceptional amount of work in their company.

You are required to act in the same manner. Always have an optimistic attitude and anticipate the greatest possible outcome. It makes no difference if you are not successful right now; what is most important is where you want to go in the future and whether or not you are ready to put in the effort to get there.

5. People that are successful have faith in their own dreams.

Do you have faith in yourself and the things you want to accomplish? Who else will believe in your goals and ambitions if you can't even believe in them yourself?

It is your dream, and you have a responsibility to safeguard it. Never believe anybody who tells you that what you want to achieve is impossible or that it can't be done. After being informed that building aeroplanes were impossible, the Wright brothers went ahead and created the first aircraft.

You have to have faith in both your aspirations and in yourself. You have to have faith that everything will turn out well for you in the end. In addition, you should always get yourself ready and start working on your goals.

Everyone has heard the saying, "No risk, no reward," but how many of us really take the risk that's required to earn the return we want? There aren't many people who can say they've accomplished this, but those who have are the ones who go on to become successful. People that are successful have not only the bravery to get started but also the fortitude to keep going. They are not only prepared to wager but also willing to "go all in" on themselves. They are not scared to sever ties with the past if it means advancing in their careers.

Obstacles encountered by females in positions of leadership.

To a greater extent or not, we are all familiar with the concept of gender equality, or at least what it refers to; yet, the pay gap is a word that is relatively unfamiliar to the general public. What exactly does "wage gap" mean? Why is it even a thing? In what ways may it be quantified? In what way does it matter? These are questions that are gaining popularity, and the fact that they are now more visible may indicate a significant step toward eliminating the problem.

Women did not begin entering the workforce in significant numbers until the 19th century, when there was an explosion in the number of industries; nevertheless, when they did so, they earned pitiful wages and worked in appallingly deplorable circumstances.

The condition in which men and women earn different amounts of money is referred to as the pay gap, and the only way to comprehend it is through the lens of gender inequality. In other words, this is just another aspect that may be traced back to gender inequality.

Women remained at home during prehistoric times to take care of the house, while males went out to get food for the family via hunting. This practice dates back to a time when humans were more primitive than they are now. Women didn't start entering the workforce in significant numbers until the industrial revolution of the 19th century, and when they did, they did so for pitiful pay and appalling working conditions. This is despite the fact that women had been around for thousands of years at this point. Jobs such as receptionists, secretaries, nurses, and teachers were some of the first to be specifically designed with the intention of catering to the interests and abilities of women as the 20th century progressed. The feminist movement eventually began to stress the importance of women obtaining an education, and a growing number of women desired a higher level of education in order to be eligible for professional-level white-collar professions. This coincided with the rise of the feminist movement. After the Spanish Civil War, which took place between 1936 and 1939, the role of women went back to a period of restricted freedom, during which they were required to ask permission from their father or possibly their spouse before leaving the country, opening a bank account, or even finding employment. In the same vein, women were prohibited from working in some professions, such as judges and notaries. It was common for unmarried women to work, but once they got married, they stopped working and saw it as a badge of honour. This was due to the fact that their husband could be the sole breadwinner and providers of the family's economic well-being, while the women could tend to the house while their husbands provided for the family's financial well-being. The pleasant, obedient, and subservient personality of the housewife was extolled as a virtue in the context of her work as a caretaker and housekeeper. There was less of a need for education, and in any event, if women were educated, it may give them an advantage when trying to find a spouse.

Although there are presently more women than males working in professional occupations, men continue to hold the most influential positions in politics and the economy.

Direct discrimination occurs when a person's pay is determined solely by their gender, despite the fact that they may possess comparable personal and professional traits. This kind of discrimination is termed the gender pay gap. It's possible that circumstances like this still come up, but the good news is that they're becoming less prevalent.

Indirect discrimination refers to the use of criteria and/or procedures that give the appearance of being neutral but ultimately result in women being placed in a worse position than males.

A wide variety of obstacles that women face, such as the glass ceiling and roles and stereotypes accepted and internalized by society, and even by women themselves, which place them at a lower rank than men in their career and personal development, contribute to wage inequality. This disparity is characterized by a very different pattern of job insertion and career paths between men and women.

Let's take a closer look at some of these challenges:

BELIEFS, ROLES, AND STEREOTYPES

Toys that are gendered have certain colours and pictures of boys or girls and use language that is more masculine or feminine, which play an important part in the early indoctrination of roles and stereotypes during childhood. It is also present in the advertisements for these toys, which make a clear reference to the roles that are perfectly classified by the toys. Additionally, it can be found in the choices that parents make for the best toys and games, which are categorized by sex. The characteristics of male games, such as action and building, are emphasized, whereas the characteristics of female games, such as caring for dolls, playing hairdressing, kitchens, and other pretty things geared at feminine jobs, are highlighted. In addition to this, it happens by promoting phrases like "boys don't cry" or "girls don't fight," behaviours that are regarded as masculine or feminine and always assigning strength and denial of sensibility to boys and glorifying the obedient, submissive attitude for girls. Last but not least, it would be unforgivable not to mention the tales in which the valour of the hero who comes to the rescue is lauded, as is the grace and submissiveness of the heroine. It would be a sin.

There are certain mentalities that are regarded as positive in men but are considered to be negative in women. Some examples of these are as follows:

In a nutshell, there is still a sexual division of labour and a lack of value assigned to the roles and values that are traditionally considered to be feminine, despite the fact that it is widely acknowledged that more women are entering the public sphere and working for pay.

A liberal education with a focus on equality, where it is not assumed that women cannot excel in technical professions that require talent in mathematics and physics, as well as a rectification in many TV programs and advertisements that objectify women, would clearly help debunk these beliefs and stereotypes, which, in the worst cases, make women the victims of physical and/or psychological violence. In addition, a rectification of many TV programs and advertisements that objectify women would help.

HORIZONTAL SEGREGATION

Throughout the course of history, parents have consistently been the carriers of these beliefs, roles, and stereotypes to their offspring. Women have traditionally been expected to be the primary caregivers for their families as well as for other individuals, whereas men have traditionally been viewed as the primary leaders, decision-makers, and communicators. As a consequence of this, we find that there is horizontal segregation in the job market; this means that women are typically found in jobs that have lower compensation and social value, and jobs are largely an extension of the activities that have traditionally and socially been assigned to each sex.

As a result, there are occupations that are regarded as being more appropriate for women, such as those in the caregiving and administrative service industries. They are undervalued and, as a result, have low wages when compared to jobs of comparable value that have higher wages precisely because they are considered to be more masculine in nature.

In Catalonia, women make up 66.2% of the workforce in the retail sector, 77.5% of the workforce in healthcare and social services, and around 70% of the workforce in cultural and sporting activities and other services.

BALANCING WORK AND FAMILY LIFE
Given that, historically and still today, women are the ones who spend the majority of their time doing housework and taking care of children or other dependent family members, this is another factor that contributes to the growing inequality in the workplace. As a result, they are required to take actions that promote lower participation in the job market, such as requesting leaves of absence and part-time workdays or interrupting their careers, in order to achieve a work-family balance that is satisfactory to them. This has a direct impact on the gender pay gap, reduces women's opportunities for promotion and employment in managerial positions, and results in lower pensions for women.

Women continue to have a lower employment rate than men and have a lower employment rate when they enter the job market; despite this, women continue to make up the majority of the population that is unemployed.

Co-responsibility, in which both men and women contribute equally to the care of their families, is the foundation of true balance. It is not irrelevant to point out that a growing number of men are becoming aware of this, particularly in the realm of child care as well as joint custody arrangements in divorces that mandate equal caretaking responsibilities. Despite this, the horizon is still quite a ways off.

In a similar vein, despite the fact that men are making strides toward and participating more in childcare, the same progress cannot be found in the care of the elderly, and women are typically the ones in charge of looking after old people. This is frequently the case as a result of divorces that involve joint custody.

WORK ON A PART-TIME BASIS

Women have a much longer and more difficult workday than men do, even though men are at their jobs for longer periods of time. This is because women are responsible for taking care of the household and the children in addition to their paid work. Women make up the majority of those hired for part-time work. According to statistics compiled by ADECA during the fourth quarter of 2016, women signed contracts for seven out of every ten part-time jobs.

Different workdays can account for a significant portion of the wage gap that exists between men and women, but this does not account for all of it.

Chapter 2

Common challenges for leaders to face

There is no guarantee that things won't fall apart around you just because you've been promoted to a leadership position in your company. Because of your status as a leader, this is entrusted specifically to your care. In fact, it is your quest if you accept it. There are always going to be challenges associated with leadership, but if you have the right strategy and the skills to go along with them, you can chart a successful course and emerge victorious.
It has been said that "if there is no struggle, there is no progress."

10 Obstacles to Effective Leadership That Every Great Leader Must Confront

The fact that you have agreed to take on a leadership position in itself constitutes a change, but every day presents new opportunities for growth and development. There are aspects of it that you have some control over, while others are entirely dependent on chance. As a leader, it is your responsibility to maintain stability in the face of shifting circumstances.

Because both of these things are going to happen, you need to be able to anticipate them and get ready for them, or you need to be able to handle them when they happen.

1. Complicated Individuals
There are bound to be some challenging individuals on your team, in your organization, and in your professional life in general. As the leader, it is your responsibility to handle them with dignity and consideration. Don't give in to their demands. You shouldn't keep exposing yourself to them for a long time. Above all else, do not allow yourself to be brought down by them.

2. Pressure
There is a great deal of pressure that is inherent in the working environment. In the long run, it will be to your advantage if you are able to acknowledge and let go of some of that pressure. You can't go at full speed one hundred per cent of the time, and if you want to be a successful leader, you need to make room in your schedule for some downtime to find some sense of equilibrium.

3. Letting Someone Go

As a leader, at some point in the future, it will be your responsibility to either suggest to them that they leave your organization or you will be required to remove someone from their position yourself. Under no circumstances should you attempt this in a hasty or angry manner. Your ability to make this organizational change for the betterment of the organization in a level-headed manner will be seen as a sign that you are a true leader.

4. Breaking some unfavourable news
Products will fail, timelines will not be met, and your goals will be behind schedule; this is all a normal part of doing business; however, it will be your responsibility to inform your board or your superiors about the situation. You will be able to figure out the next steps to take if you have the ability to break bad news calmly and clearly, without resorting to drama. Things can go wrong, but how you handle them moving forward is going to determine how far you go from here.

5. Maintaining a Positive Attitude
As a leader, you will inevitably experience times when you feel your motivation for the project or the organization waning. It happens to the best of us, but what you need to do is muster all o the good stuff around you and get back on track after it has happened. If you can't find a solution to the problem, there's no point in wasting time worrying about it. You will not always be the number one cheerleader in your own mind; however, your team is expecting you to be, so get out there and share the enthusiasm that you do have, even when you are a little off your game.

6. Culture Issues
There is no reason to believe that the fact that you work for a company eliminates any problems associated with your own personal culture. It's possible that your office is the type that has trouble working together as a team, struggles with

communication, engages in gossip, or has members who try to bring others down. You, as the leader, are going to be responsible for addressing whatever this issue is. It is not simple to alter the cultural practices of an organization, but you are the one who sets the tone. If you don't want other people to gossip about you, don't gossip about other people. You need to be able to work well with teams if you want to see improved collaboration among group efforts. You are the one who will ultimately determine how the culture in your organization actually functions.

"Until the employees love the company first, the customers will never love the company," customers will never love a company. – Simon Sinek

7. Being Respected and Liked at the Same Time
There will be times when people do not like you. The moment you put your hand up to lead something, someone else will try to knock you off the leadership position. That is the way life is. To avoid being swayed by that, you should strive to communicate in a way that is both kind and focused. You will eventually earn people's respect, and if you're lucky, you might even win their favour.

8. Keeping One's Attention Centered
It is so simple to let one's mind wander! Everyone is either trying to sell you something, get your attention, or get something from you. Everyone wants something. That is a necessary step in acknowledging your leadership responsibilities. Your job is to keep your attention on the prize at hand and not let yourself be sidetracked by anything that

catches your eye. You are in charge of leading a team, delivering a product, or finishing a project; therefore, you must make a plan, keep your head down, and keep your focus.

9. Difficulties in Communicating
Someone on the team is going to miss the deadline, someone else is going to reply to an email that they shouldn't have, and someone else still isn't going to get the memo altogether. These are all things that are going to happen in inevitably. As a leader, problems with communication are likely the source of the majority of your stress. Your efforts to hone your abilities to communicate in a straightforward and succinct manner will be beneficial to the entire organization.

10. Handling a Dud
Every once in a while, a project or an event ends up being a complete failure for no apparent reason. Don't be concerned. It is inevitable that some of us will experience it. What matters is how you choose to deal with it. Don't give your team any room to wallow in self-pity or point the finger at others. Don't beat yourself up over it; instead, pick yourself up and figure out how to make the next thing even better.

Shouldering responsibility is a significant component of leadership, even though it isn't the only aspect of leadership that involves dealing with challenging situations. Every time you are forced to contend with something challenging, you are providing yourself with an opportunity to learn how to handle similar situations in the future. Your development as a leader will be directly proportional to the lessons you learn about navigating both positive and negative experience.

Chapter 3

Conquering your own self-doubt and the imposter syndrome

Consider some of your most notable accomplishments. Do you have a sense of accomplishment about the things you've done? Or do you feel like a fraud?

Does it fill you with joy whenever you get a raise, a promotion, or an accolade? Or does it come with the fear that one day your secret will be revealed, and everyone will find out that you were just lucky?

You might be surprised to find out that you are in good company if you experience feelings of inadequacy and self-doubt. Many people struggle with similar issues. Impostor syndrome is something that typically affects people who are very successful. If this sounds familiar to you, take heart: there's a good chance that you're actually more competent than you give yourself credit for. Genuine con artists aren't concerned with details like this.

In this article, we will discuss Impostor Syndrome, including what it is, how it can cause you to restrict your options and the solutions that are available to help you overcome it.

Applying these tactics will help you silence the voice of your inner critic.

What is meant by the term "impostor syndrome"?

The overwhelming sensation that you don't deserve your success is a symptom of impostor syndrome, which is also referred to as impostorism, the impostor phenomenon, and the fraud syndrome. You start to believe the lie that you are not as intelligent, creative, or talented as others might think you are. And you have the sneaking suspicion that your successes are the result of pure good fortune, impeccable timing, or simply being "in the right place at the right time."

It's possible that you frequently doubt your capabilities or ask yourself, "What gives me the right?" in these situations. It's possible that you'll even get the sense that you don't belong there at all. Your greatest concern is that you will be discovered to be a liar at some point in the future.

It's possible that Impostor Syndrome is connected to other forms of self-doubt, like the fear of succeeding, the fear of failing, or even self-sabotaging. However, the issue isn't just a lack of self-confidence or an excessive amount of humility. It involves an ongoing fear of being found out, of being alone, and of being rejected.

The onset of impostor syndrome frequently coincides with significant life changes, such as the beginning of a new job, the receipt of an award or promotion, or the assumption of additional responsibilities, such as teaching others, launching one's own business, or becoming a parent for the first time.

Because of your self-perceived shortcomings, you might believe that you need to exert more effort in order to prevent yourself from being "unmasked." It's possible that this will lead to even more success and recognition, but it'll also make you feel like an even bigger fraud. However, "downshifting" can frequently be a consequence of an inaccurate assessment of one's abilities. This is the point at which you reevaluate your objectives and lower your standards for success, which prevents you from realizing your full potential.

people with high abilities frequently have a low awareness of those abilities. On the other hand, this does not imply that all of them suffer from impostor syndrome, which is characterized by a unique fear of being "discovered."

The Impostor Syndrome, Regardless of Gender or Race

It has been believed for a long time that women are more likely to suffer from impostor syndrome than men, particularly in settings that are dominated by men. However, results of recent studies have demonstrated that it has an equal impact on people of both sexes. The likelihood of experiencing symptoms of impostor syndrome is higher among members of ethnic minority groups. Furthermore, those who experience symptoms of impostor syndrome are frequently also affected by symptoms of anxiety or depression.

Should I Be Worried That I May Have Impostor Syndrome?

Let's take a look at some of the most common signs and symptoms of impostor syndrome now:

- **A sense of inadequacy and persistent self-doubt**

The impostor syndrome manifests itself in the form of a profound lack of self-assurance. When you achieve success, you can find yourself thinking, "I'm not worthy," or "I don't deserve this," and these are both negative thoughts.

The majority of individuals will, at some point in their life, have low self-confidence, but those affected by impostor syndrome have this sensation all the time, and it is severe.

- **displaying characteristics of a perfectionist**

People who strive for perfection are more likely to suffer from impostor syndrome. When you fail to achieve the unreasonable standards you set for yourself, you may experience feelings of embarrassment or disappointment. When you strive for perfection, it's possible you'll never be happy with the things you've accomplished, and you're more likely to dwell on the errors and setbacks you've encountered.

This type of thinking has been responsible for the downfall of even the most accomplished people. For instance, the winner of the 2019 World Heptathlon, Katarina Johnson-Thompson, has admitted that she has struggled with persistent self-doubt, even though she has competed at an extremely high level. In a similar manner, former First Lady of the United States Michelle Obama has discussed how, despite her numerous accomplishments, she continues to struggle with Impostor Syndrome and how it can be especially challenging for women of colour to conquer this condition.

- **Steering Clear of Responsibility**

Some persons who suffer from impostor syndrome have a tendency toward perfectionism, whereas others with the condition have the opposite tendency. You can have such a crippling fear of failing that it prevents you from taking on additional duties, applying for new jobs, or even agreeing to accept promotions.

Because you are afraid of making mistakes, you could find it difficult to speak up in meetings or answer questions without first consulting with another person. This could make it difficult for you to participate. This could drive you to put off working on things that you know you need to complete because you are afraid of getting negative feedback on your performance. Alternatively, it could induce you to avoid working on those chores altogether.

- **Concerned About Being Found Out And Judged**

One of the most common symptoms of impostor syndrome is a persistent worry of being "discovered." You are not only plagued by the dread that you are not good enough but you are also terrified that your coworkers and supervisors will discover that you are a phoney – if they haven't already done so before. This fear is keeping you up at night.

This fear could even drive you to do irrational and extreme things. It's possible that, in an effort to avoid "exposure," you drive yourself to your physical and mental breaking point while simultaneously refusing to acknowledge that the quality of your work is sufficient. This can lead to a vicious cycle of effort, unhappiness, and dread, which may further harm your self-esteem and cause you to feel less confident in yourself.

- **Negating Your Own Potential for Success**

You probably minimize the impact of your successes a great deal. You may discover that you are frequently caught up in negative self-talk that leaves you with the impression that you do not merit the achievement that you have achieved.

You have the propensity to dismiss your achievements as "easy," despite the fact that you have invested a significant amount of time and effort into achieving them. If you've been requested to deliver a presentation, for instance, you might think, "What am I going to say?" "Where do I get the authority to speak my mind? Why should anybody pay attention to what I have to say?"

And despite the fact that you do receive great feedback, you have a tendency to create excuses to ignore it. For instance, you could tell yourself, "Well, I guess I just got lucky and had a lot of people helping me." It's also possible that you believe that if you started over, you wouldn't have the same amount of luck, talent, or talents that led to your current level of success.
Do Members of My Team Have Impostor Syndrome?

The persons who have impostor syndrome aren't the only ones who are harmed by this condition. It is also detrimental to the businesses and sports teams to which they belong. Therefore, if you are in a position of leadership, it is in your best interest to keep an eye out for members of your team who are battling feelings of inadequacy.

They could refuse promotions or avoid taking on demanding new jobs or participate in high-profile projects. They are prone to feel awkward when complimented or praised, especially if they are told that their good work or success is due to luck or that they know the right people.

One further warning indication is when the individual makes unfavourable comparisons to other people and uses self-deprecating phrases like "I'm not sure I know what I'm talking about, but..." or "It might just be me, but..." in their conversations. They might even admit out loud that they are afraid of failing or appearing incompetent.

- **Overcoming the Feeling That You Are a Fraud**

Realizing that you suffer from impostor syndrome is frequently the most challenging step in resolving the condition. There is a widespread misconception that the alternative is to behave in a pompous and self-important manner; however, this does not have to be the case.

If you believe that you suffer from the condition known as "Impostor Syndrome," the following six tactics can assist you in overcoming it:

1. Acknowledge and Accept Your Emotions

The first thing you need to do is acknowledge what you're feeling and why you're feeling it.
To get started, you should keep a journal. Write down your thoughts and emotions of inadequacy or self-doubt whenever you have them, and be as clear as possible about why you are having these thoughts and feelings. There is a good probability that when you see your thoughts written down in black and white, you will be able to recognize how destructive they actually are, and most importantly, you will be able to fight them!
Keep in mind that although your feelings are very significant, they are still only feelings and may not always accurately reflect the world around you. Simply because you lack confidence in your abilities does not mean that this is the case.

For instance, you might write in your notebook, "I delivered a presentation to the board, and although they claimed I did very well, I could sense that they weren't impressed." This would be an accurate representation of their feelings. If you give some thought to what you've written and how the board members truly reacted to what you said, you'll most likely come to the conclusion that their reaction was genuine and that your worries were unwarranted.

The next step is to practice cognitive restructuring in order to combat the negative thoughts and feelings that arise automatically. Put your negative thoughts to rest by writing down some positive mantras or affirmations and rereading them regularly. You might say something like, "I am a confident, capable professional," or "I will be successful because I know what I'm doing." Both of these statements are true.

2. Interact with Other People

Reach out and have conversations with people you respect. It is possible that a surprising number of your friends and coworkers can empathize with how you are currently feeling. Listen to the advice of the individuals you hold in high regard in your life, and allow them to demonstrate to you how your concerns are unwarranted.

3. Formulate a plan for immediate action.

Dealing with impostor syndrome requires sustained effort, but there are times when you need strategies to help you cope with the syndrome during exceptionally difficult situations. Try to combat negative self-talk by removing yourself from the emotional strength of the voice when it begins to take control of your thoughts.

Imagine you are talking about yourself to someone else. Try reversing your train of thought and asking yourself, "Why did they do that?" rather than "Why did I do that?" Because of this, you will be able to acquire a more objective perspective on the issue, as well as on your own ideas and feelings.

Take on greater challenges in order to combat negative thoughts such as "I'm not good enough." It may at first appear counterintuitive, but if you take risks that you can control and are successful with them, you can build a case against the critical voice in your head.

4. Recognize both Your Capabilities and Your Limitations

Gaining a better understanding of both your strong and weak points is a great way to boost your self-confidence. Carry out a personal SWOT analysis to figure out where your strengths lie and where weaknesses lie, then consider how you might improve upon your areas of weakness.

When you have a more in-depth understanding of your strong points and weak points, you won't have to spend as much time worrying that you aren't qualified for certain activities, projects, or roles. This will free up more of your time. Create a support system consisting of people who inspire you and in whom you can have complete faith to assist you in overcoming your critical inner voice.

5. Get Over Your Obsession with Perfection

Conquer your tendency toward perfectionism by giving yourself frequent breaks, practising methods of relaxation, and keeping your eye on the broader picture.

Figure out how to develop objectives for yourself that are both attainable and hard at the same time. It is important to keep in mind that making errors is an inevitable part of living and that it is not the end of the world if you are unable to achieve a particular objective or submit something on time.

In point of fact, errors are evidence that you are not scared to take chances and that you are pushing yourself to attempt new things. Consider your failures to be valuable learning experiences that will help you do even better the following time around rather than embarrassing setbacks that you should be ashamed of making.

6. Take Credit for Your Achievements

People who suffer from impostor syndrome have a difficult time accepting praise. When things go well for them, they tend to credit their accomplishments to external circumstances such as the assistance of others or good fortune. However, whenever something goes wrong, they have a tendency to take full responsibility for it.

Make an effort to strengthen the internal centre of control you have over your life. If you believe that your actions, choices, and decisions impact the course of your life, then you are able to accept responsibility for both the successes and failures that you have experienced in your life. Therefore, the next time you accomplish a goal or complete an important assignment, make sure you give yourself credit for the skills and talents that helped you get there.

Remember to take some time to savour and rejoice in your accomplishments as well. You should maintain a log of the compliments and good feedback that you get. And remember to bring it to mind the next time that critical voice in your head makes an appearance. This will help to lessen the impact of any criticism that you are levelling at yourself and will give you a much-needed boost of confidence.

Chapter 4

Building self-confidence in yourself and your team

It is not possible to acquire confidence in the same way that one can learn a set of rules; rather, confidence is a state of mind. Think positively, get some practice, get some training, increase your knowledge, and talk to other people; these are all great techniques to build or strengthen your levels of confidence.

Your sense of well-being, your acceptance of your body and mind (your level of self-esteem), and your belief in your own ability, abilities, and experience are all necessary components of confidence. The majority of people harbour a secret desire to improve their level of self-assurance.

How would you define self-confidence?
In spite of the fact that self-confidence can have a variety of meanings to various individuals, in practice, what it really means is having faith in oneself.
Our upbringing and the lessons we've learned play a role in developing our sense of self-assurance to some extent. These teachings have an impact on the things that we believe about ourselves as well as the beliefs that we hold about other people. We learn how to think about ourselves and how to

behave with other people. Our life experiences, as well as the ways in which we've learned to respond to a variety of circumstances, both contribute to our level of confidence.
The level of one's self-confidence is not a constant measure. Our confidence in our ability to carry out jobs and responsibilities as well as respond appropriately to events might fluctuate, and some days we may feel more confident than others.

Fear of the unknown, criticism, being uncomfortable with physical appearance (low self-esteem), feeling unprepared, poor time management, a lack of information and previous failures are some of the causes that might contribute to low levels of confidence. Other contributing variables include: When we do not have confidence in ourselves, it is because we are concerned about what other people will think of us. Should we make a mistake, there is a good chance that others may mock us, complain, or make fun of us. This line of thinking can keep us from doing things that we need to do or things that we want to accomplish because we may assume that the repercussions will be too embarrassing or painful.
An unhealthy amount of confidence can be problematic if it leads a person to believe that they are capable of accomplishing anything, even if they lack the essential skills, abilities, and knowledge to perform the task successfully. In these kinds of circumstances, having an excessive amount of confidence might lead to failure. When you are extremely confident, you run the risk of coming off to other people as arrogant or egotistical. This is especially true if you are a leader. If people have the impression that you are arrogant,

there is a lot greater chance that they will take delight in your failure.

Associated Domains
The terms "confidence" and "self-esteem" are frequently used interchangeably. However, they do not refer to the same thing. The way we feel about our capacity to carry out duties, functions, and tasks is what we mean when we talk about having confidence in ourselves. The way that we feel about ourselves, how we look, how we think, and whether or not we believe that we are worthwhile or valuable all contribute to our self-esteem. Those who have poor self-esteem frequently also struggle with a lack of general confidence, but it is possible for people who have healthy self-esteem to simultaneously have low confidence. It is also completely feasible for persons who have poor self-esteem to be extremely confident in certain areas. This is something that is perfectly possible.

To confidently play a part or finish a task, it is not necessary to eliminate the possibility of making errors. Making mistakes is unavoidable, particularly when attempting anything for the first time. Knowing what to do when faults are brought to light is an important component of confidence; as a result, confidence also involves problem-solving and decision-making.

Methods for Increasing One's Self-Assurance
Improving one's confidence can be approached from two different angles. Even if the end goal is for you to feel more confident in who you are and what you're capable of, it's

important to remember that other people will judge you based on how you present yourself to them.

The list that follows has many suggestions as to how to accomplish this goal.

The Activities of Planning and Preparation

When confronted with something unfamiliar or potentially challenging, people frequently report feeling less confident. The ability to plan for and get yourself ready for the unknown is probably the single most significant aspect of establishing confidence.

For instance, if you are interested in a new job and have an interview scheduled, it is in your best interest to prepare for the meeting. Prepare what you want to say and think about the questions that you might be asked in advance. You should run through your responses with some friends or coworkers and get their comments.

There are a lot of other ways to prepare for an interview. Maybe you should stop by the salon before you leave and get your hair done. How are you planning on getting to the interview, and how long do you anticipate the trip will take? What should you put on today? Take control of unknown situations to the best of your ability, divide tasks into smaller sub-tasks, and plan as many of the tasks as you can.

In certain circumstances, it may be necessary to also have backup plans or contingency plans in the event that your primary plan does not succeed. If you had intended to drive to the interview, but when you got there, the car wouldn't start, what other means of transportation could you use to get there?

Being able to respond rationally and calmly to unexpected events is a sign of confidence.

Learning and doing research can help us feel more confident about our ability to take on different roles, responsibilities, and tasks in our lives.

Your awareness will increase if you are aware of what to anticipate as well as how and why things are done. This will, in most cases, make you feel more prepared and, ultimately, more confident.

When this happens, we need to combine our knowledge with experience so that we can regain our previous level of self-assurance regarding our capacity to carry out the roles and responsibilities that have been assigned to us. Putting what we have learned in the classroom into practice helps us become more self-assured while also enhancing our capacity to learn and comprehend new material.

Expectant parents who have never done this before are likely to experience anxiety and a lack of self-assurance about becoming parents for the first time. It is likely that they will purchase books or go online to websites that provide guidance and explain some of the mysteries. They are also likely to talk to other parents in order to increase their knowledge and comprehension.

Training may be provided for employees at their places of employment so that they can learn how to manage or work with new procedures and systems. This is of utmost significance during times of organizational change because a lot of people have a natural tendency to fight against change. If, on the other hand, those who will be impacted by the changes are provided with sufficient information and training, then such resistance can typically be minimized because the staff will feel more prepared and, as a result, more confident with the new system.

How to Encourage Confidence in Others and Create Teams That Are Self-Assured

Imagine you are watching a sporting event between two teams, one of which is more confident than the other team.

The members of the more self-assured squad are aware that they have a decent possibility of coming out on top in the competition. As a direct consequence of this, every member of the team is able to make sound judgments, and the players are able to collaborate effectively. In the meantime, the other team's confidence is beginning to waver. Players have difficulty believing in their own abilities, which leads to hesitation and a reluctance to commit fully to any one course of action.

When something like this occurs, the team with the most self-assurance will most likely come out on top.

In the workplace, the same guiding principles should be followed. When members of your team lack self-confidence, it can prevent them from realizing their full potential as individuals and as a group. Because of this, it is essential to build the confidence of those around us, particularly if we are in a position of leadership over a group.

Understanding the Role of Low Self-Confidence

People who struggle with a lack of self-confidence merely succeed in life. They see more potential dangers than opportunities, they do not perform particularly well in novel circumstances, and they frequently have a low opinion of themselves. In addition to this, they hardly ever put their faith in their own discretion, and they are likely to attribute any successes they do have to good fortune rather than to the efforts they put in themselves.

People who have a high level of self-confidence, on the other hand, are frequently more productive and effective, and they have the ability to boost the morale of the entire group. They are also more comfortable taking risks, which can have positive implications for both their individual careers and the teams on which they play.

People's chances of succeeding in accomplishing their objectives are greatly influenced by their level of confidence. Follow the steps below to help a member of your team improve their self-confidence once you've determined that they are suffering from a lack of self-assurance.

Develop Knowledge and Skills

There is a good chance that you rely on a number of different skills in order to do a good job at your job. What results can you anticipate from the successful application of these skills? You feel confident! You have developed these abilities over the course of your career, and you are confident in your ability to apply them to the challenge at hand.

The very same can be said about the members of your team. They are going to experience increased self-assurance in direct proportion to the breadth and depth of their skill set.

Therefore, one effective method for boosting the self-assurance of members of your team is to foster an environment that is conducive to learning and to make a number of opportunities for additional instruction available to them. People's sense of self-assurance will increase in direct proportion to the amount of knowledge and expertise they bring to their jobs, particularly when they are confronted with difficult tasks or projects.

Establish Objectives for Yourself.

The successful completion of tasks and projects can provide a boost of confidence for many people. But this self-assurance can only be achieved when individuals are aware of the steps they should take.

For this reason, it is of the utmost importance to set distinct objectives for each and every member of your team. Goals are what define success, and they provide individuals with a target to work toward. Without them, they are labouring without any clear purpose.

Consequently, it is your responsibility to ensure that the members of your team are aware of the objectives toward which they are working and to assist them in accomplishing these objectives. Then, once they have accomplished what they set out to do, rejoice in their success!

Identify "Triggers"

There are not many people who can say that they are completely self-confident, and the majority of people would like to improve their self-confidence in certain aspects of their lives.

We might experience a lack of confidence whenever we are confronted with a new challenge or when we are asked to do something that we would rather not do. There is a possibility that things won't go as planned, that our performance won't live up to expectations, and that we will emerge from this with a negative reputation.

If you work with someone who suffers from low self-confidence, you should assist them in determining the "trigger situations" that bring on their symptoms. They will be able to focus on building the information and abilities they need to feel more confident after they have identified the factors that cause their confidence to waver.

Asking them to develop a list of all the job scenarios that make them feel confident is the first step in doing this. This could be anything from contributing to the company blog to assisting with the development of the budget for your department. This list should include everything that brings them joy and boosts their sense of self-assurance.

Then you should have them think about the reasons why they feel confident in each of these situations. What is it that they know or are able to do that gives them a sense of accomplishment?

Next, you should have them make a list of the circumstances in which they do not feel confident. This may include delivering presentations, voicing a viewpoint at meetings, or composing a report. Why do they not feel secure when confronted with these challenges? What fresh information and capabilities might make them feel more confident in each situation?

Finding out what these triggers are may be an eye-opening experience in and of itself. However, if they are aware of the areas in which they may need improvement, they will be more driven to confront their phobias.

Empower Others While You Delegate

It is imperative that you give your team the freedom to make their own choices if you want them to tackle tasks with self-assurance. This will allow you to achieve the confidence you seek from your team.

When you give your people the authority to decide what tasks need to be completed, you will notice that they begin to take ownership of the work that they do. It is now entirely their job, and when they are successful, it may do wonders for their self-confidence.

Delegate responsibilities to your employees and empower them to make their own choices whenever you have the opportunity to do so. Your members will feel more empowered after you demonstrate that you have faith in their decisions and abilities by delegating more responsibility to them. This will demonstrate that you trust their judgment and competence.

Be aware, however, that people who have low self-confidence may resist this at first: after all, they may doubt that they will make the right decisions. People who have low self-confidence may resist this because they doubt that they will make the right decisions. Encourage them to start on manageable and relatively straightforward assignments, so you can combat these doubts. Then, if they depend on you an excessive amount for assistance or direction, you should push them to become more autonomous. They will be forced to make their own judgments as a result of this rather than coming to you for assistance or counsel.

Celebrate Success

Recognizing and celebrating one's accomplishments is a proven way to boost one's sense of well-being and confidence; thus, it is essential that we all do so.

Celebrate with your team whenever they achieve a crucial objective or attain a goal they've been working toward. Reward them with a supper as a group, or better yet, give each person a pair of tickets to an event you know they'll appreciate. At the absolute least, you should express your delight at their accomplishment and let them know how much you value the efforts they have put out.

It is also essential to maintain your team's enthusiasm for the work that they are doing. Celebrating success helps with this, but keeping motivation high long-term is key to building a team with high confidence levels. You can find additional information on this topic in our article that discusses the Sirota Three-Factor Theory. This theory explains the significance of fairness, achievement, and a sense of camaraderie in the process of motivating people.

Inspire Optimism and Positive Thinking
Many people who lack self-confidence focus on negative thoughts. They might have thoughts such as "I am not clever enough" or "I am unable to do it." People who have these negative beliefs fall more and deeper into a downward cycle, which reinforces their perception that they will never be good enough to achieve. Of course, this just makes the situation much more difficult!

Inspire individuals to think positively and give affirmations by encouraging them to utilize them. One technique is to show them how to "flip their thoughts" – every time they catch themselves thinking a negative thought, teach them to think its rational opposite.

As an example, if individuals believe that "They should instead think, "I know I have the knowledge and abilities to do this assignment," instead of saying something like, "I'm not clever enough to finish this project." In the event that I do need assistance, I can always ask for it."

When we change bad thinking into a good idea, we bring about a subtle alteration in our thoughts. Because the shift in our perspective and energy is nearly physical, using this strategy may have a significant impact on our level of self-assurance.

Finding a Happy Medium Between Self-Confidence and Excessive Confidence
When individuals improve their level of self-confidence, there is always the possibility that they may develop an unhealthy level of overconfidence or even arrogance. There is no question that there is a thin line in this situation; nonetheless, once that line has been crossed, the morale and productivity of the group may begin to suffer as a result of the actions of these individuals. The worst thing that may happen is for individuals to become negligent because they have an inflated opinion of their own capacity to improvise in challenging circumstances.

If this occurs to a member of your team, the first step is to bring the matter to that person's notice in a non-threatening way. There is a good chance that they are unaware that their behaviour has reached the level of arrogance. Have a one-on-one conversation with them, be specific about what it is that they are saying or doing, and describe the reasons why their actions could be interpreted as arrogance.

Make sure you communicate with the individual and let them know if the team has become tense or angry as a result of their actions. People are often driven to change when they become aware that their actions are negatively impacting the lives of others.

Chapter 5

Regain Control of Your Time and Energy

It doesn't matter who you are or where you live; the one thing that we all have in common is that we enjoy daydreaming, which is when we close our eyes and pretend that we're already leading the life that we were always meant to lead. It's a want that's hardwired into our very selves. A desire for more. Make more progress. Become more.

It is for this reason that we launch new companies, write books, learn to play instruments, get master's degrees, switch careers, and learn to cook, sew, or speak Swahili.

We are all in pursuit of a dream, including dreams associated with our daily lives. Such as finding a place to call home, someone to love, or a way to find inner peace; being in good health; being financially independent; experiencing simple happiness; etc. Maybe it's just a life with less agony, less heartache, and less time spent alone.

Dreams are not only what contribute to making the world a better place but also what contribute to making you and me better people. Every opportunity that presents itself, the two of us ought to go after our dreams. Thankfully, the majority of us do, and we mean it with all of our hearts.

Unfortuitously, a significant number of us lose up on such aspirations practically before we even begin, shoving them to the back of our sock drawers until we forget they were ever there.

It is simple to find reasons to justify the failure of our aspirations. We are unable to begin because we do not have the necessary resources, including time, money, expertise, or dedication. However, the true foe is more subversive and sneaky than we could have ever imagined.

Simply put, we've reached our limit. We don't have the strength to pursue our goals.

There is always someplace to go and some activity to participate in. Late meetings at work, having to drive the carpool, having to make lunches, having to take out the garbage, and having schoolwork to accomplish.

We end up with a cold. Lose our job. Commence a romantic connection. Put an end to the connection. Birthdays. Holidays. Appointments with the dentist The list may go on forever and is really tiring. It's no surprise that our options for a better life are completely exhausted at this point. It's all we can do to keep up with our current lives at this point.

Money is not the most important medium of exchange in our day. It is energy. Energy is both the kind that allows us to get out of bed and the kind that inspires us to improve our lives and the world around us; if we don't have the strength to follow our goals, even the most admirable aspirations in the world amount to nothing.

Meniere's disease is a condition that affects the inner ear, and I was given that diagnosis a few years ago. After another two months, I went to the doctor and was told that I had a benign growth called an acoustic neuroma in the opposite ear.

Despite the fact that none of these ailments is deadly and that there are undoubtedly individuals with conditions that are considerably more severe than mine, I discovered that I was in the uncommon situation of being weary all the time.

I think I could get used to the symptoms. Dizziness. Vertigo. The ears are full of ringing. Hearing impairment But the fact that I was spent, exhausted, and lacking in energy was the true adversary in my struggle. I had no interest in pursuing the things that had been significant to me in the past.

At the same time, I was going through a transition in my profession, which took even more of my energy. In addition to this, I had terrible dietary habits, which further depleted my energy levels.

The thing with energy is that it can leave us in so many different ways, and that's the thing about it. Having poor health might be a contributing factor, but so can being in an unhealthy relationship, being unable to make your mortgage payments, or learning that your child is being harassed at school. Worry. Fear. Regret. Anger. They are all energy busters that work like a "pin in the balloon."

There is, thankfully, cause for optimism. An abundance of hope. Simply put, we need to find out how to restore our energy levels. The struggle to recapture our energy is, in point of fact, one of the essential wars we'll ever engage in. If we are successful here, we will earn the strength necessary to fight an even more significant battle—the struggle for our aspirations and the life that we have envisaged for ourselves.

Obviously, regaining control of our energy is not something that can be accomplished by chance, and it is not always simple. However, each new day presents us with priceless possibilities to replenish our energy stores. Here are some random tips to get started.

You just need to choose one and go on with it. It makes no difference which one you choose. It doesn't matter who it is. Then you should try one more. And yet another. You won't even realize it, but before you know it, you'll have the strength to recover the life you've always wanted. That restores our strength and vitality.

But you'll need to put in some deliberate effort and have a curious mindset to succeed. We need to be watchful, keeping a watchful eye both on ourselves and on the world around us at all times, seeking those tidbits of wisdom and patterns of behaviour that will refresh our spirits.

It is the only way that any of us can ever be strong enough to pursue our aspirations and live the lives that were intended for us to live.

Dream away, but make sure that one of your first dreams is to give someone the gift of energy.

Your better self in the future will be grateful to you for it.

Chapter 6

The common strategies used by the most successful women in the world

The following are ten trade secrets of very successful female business owners, which we hope will encourage and inspire you to launch and expand your own company right now.

1. NO MORE TALKING AND DREAMING, ONLY DOING!

First up is a secret that was shared by Miki Agrawal, who has been (co) the founder of three successful firms. Her idea is rather straightforward: Stay true to yourself while also challenging anything that doesn't seem to make sense to you. Her recommendation is as simple as her outlook: Just get stuff done.

Even though it seems to be straightforward, we are aware that this is not the case. In point of fact, it is not easy to silence the critical voice in your head and put an end to daydreaming about what your life may be like in the future. But this is the key to how Miki Agrawal was able to achieve her objectives: she focused on doing one or two things each day and worked her way up to her ultimate goal step by step.

2. BE SURE TO LOOK AT THINGS FROM A NEW (CHILDLIKE) PERSPECTIVE!

This is another insightful piece of business counsel offered by the successful entrepreneur Miki Agrawal. Because of this particular pattern of behaviour, she was able to think up an original and straightforward concept for a product that she called "Tushy."

She had just given some consideration to the widespread practice of washing the buttocks with paper, and she has come to the conclusion that this is not an adequate level of cleanliness. As a result, she came up with the idea for the "Tushy," a device that can be used in any toilet and rinses the buttocks with water.

When you look at the world through the eyes of a kid, you are more likely to wonder about everyday occurrences that an adult would never consider.

3.It takes a village to raise a child, and you can't do it all by yourself.

This little-known fact was divulged to me by Delia Fischer, one of the co-founders of the thriving German web firm Westwing. She and her coworkers came up with the idea of offering customers the ability to purchase upscale yet reasonably priced home decor online.

During an interview, Delia Fischer stated that the misconception that she must be responsible for all aspects of her business was the most significant error she had made as an entrepreneur. In point of fact, it may be preferable to simply request the assumption of responsibility from an individual who has more expertise in a certain area of the company.

If you insist on doing everything by yourself, you can end yourself producing work that is low in quality and unprofessional, both of which are detrimental to your chances of being successful. Therefore, if you are in need of assistance, seek it out!

4. UNPLUGGING, RECHARGING, AND RENEWING YOURSELF IMPROVES PERFORMANCE

Arianna Huffington, who is an entrepreneur, is widely considered to be one of the most successful women in the world. In 2003, she established the online magazine known as "The Huffington Post," and in 2011, she sold it for more than $300 million.

Her primary piece of advice for achieving success is to sometimes move away from one's responsibilities, disconnect from electronic devices, recharge, and refresh oneself, as required. She claims that this particular practice may boost performance even more than putting in a lot of effort would.

In general, Arianna Huffington believes that leading a healthy lifestyle is the most important factor in one's level of success. She highlights the good influence that sleep has had on her daily productivity and sleeps for around eight hours each and every day.

5. HAVING THE CORRECT PEOPLE ON STAFF IS THE KEY TO SUCCESS.

This tip was provided by Claudia Helming, the woman who established the German online marketplace DaWanda, which specializes in handcrafted goods. She places a strong emphasis on the fact that in order to be successful in business, it is not necessary to know everything. It is not necessary for you to have the ability to design software programs or construct webshops in order to build an empire in the realm of electronic commerce.

The most important thing is to make connections with competent professionals who are able to carry out these responsibilities on your behalf. What you can and cannot accomplish is entirely up to you! Because of this, the key is to not be terrified of starting a company that you can't start all by yourself and instead embrace the challenge

6. PERSISTENCE IS THE MOST IMPORTANT FACTOR INVOLVED IN YOUR SUCCESS.

You probably were prepared for that one since everyone in the start-up sector is always repeating it; thus, the fact that it is true is no longer a secret. Nevertheless, we do not want to conceal this significant piece of guidance, which comes from such a successful female entrepreneur as Kathryn Minshew, co-founder and CEO of the career platform known as "The Muse."

Following the launch of "The Muse" in 2011, the company expanded rapidly to become an empire in the field of professional development and has successfully secured $28 million in capital.

She acknowledged, in the course of an interview, that the primary factors that contributed to her success were perseverance and the capacity to find a way around any hurdle. Her trick is to constantly look for a way to make things work that you are passionate about, even if it seems impossible.

7. DO NOT TRY TO BE SOMEONE ELSE'S VERSION OF WHAT SUCCESS LOOKS LIKE

This piece of guidance, which is more of a hint than a secret but is nevertheless essential, was provided once again by Kathryn Minshew. It is counterproductive to engage in the practice of attempting to modify your style, image, or attitude just because you believe that this is how you should be in order to be successful.

Because of what other people said to her, Kathryn Minshew had her own reservations about the value of her great intuitive abilities in the business world. It took her a long time and a change of profession before she realized that this quality set her apart from others and helped contribute to her achievements.

8. The most successful innovations are often strange in some way.

Morgan DeBaun, a woman entrepreneur, is the creator of the online platform known as "Blavity." This platform was developed both by and for black millennials. This secret has a lot of weight for her since, at the beginning of her endeavour, she had to contend with a lot of criticism.

People have voiced their concerns that the target audience is insufficiently large and that the name is peculiar sounding. Even individuals with a lot of expertise were critical of the notion and predicted that it would fail. Morgan DeBaun was first worried as a result of these remarks; nevertheless, she quickly came to the realization that the finest ideas are sometimes a bit strange and that this should not be a cause to abandon the project. The movie "Blavity" demonstrates that unconventional ideas may be profitable provided their backers have strong convictions in their potential.

9. You may learn the most unbelievable life skills through debating and cold-calling other people.

Because cold calling is so commonly seen as employment for those of lesser social standing, this hidden fact may at first seem to be strange. As a result, Sara Blakely, who is the youngest self-made female millionaire in the United States, thinks that cold-calling and arguing should be fundamental skills for anybody working in the business.

Why? Because you get experience in making sales. It teaches you to be resolute and to go on regardless of the circumstances, particularly when other people are cruel or unfriendly to you. Participating in debate pushes you to think fast on your feet and to explain your thoughts in a way that is crystal clear. When used in the context of product sales, each of these soft talents may help your company achieve greater levels of success.

10. WHEN YOUR BUSINESS IS EXPANDING QUICKLY, THE MOST IMPORTANT CHALLENGE IS TO RECRUIT STAFF QUICKLY ENOUGH.

The next piece of advice comes from Natalie Ellis, who is the creator of a website called "Bossbabe." Boss babe is a network of ambitious young women and a platform for female business owners. As a result of the rapid expansion of her company, she made the error of hiring someone very rapidly just because she believed she should.

Finding the proper individuals to go on this incredible trip with you might be challenging, but doing so is very vital to your chances of succeeding in any endeavour you undertake. When you get to that stage, be sure to keep it in mind!

Ten business strategies used by eight very successful women; have any of them inspired you? I really hope that you were able to take in all of the incredible information and advice that was presented and that you will be able to use some of it in the future when you are developing your company.

Conclusion

Always think optimistically, have optimistic thoughts, take persistent action, never give up, and always dream big. Most importantly, believe in yourself and your ambitions.

www.ingramcontent.com/pod-product-compliance
Lightning Source LLC
Chambersburg PA
CBHW050311220526
45465CB00005B/1948